Animals of Africa

by Siobhan Phillips

PEARSON

Glenview, Illinois • Boston, Massachusetts • Chandler, Arizona
Upper Saddle River, New Jersey

giraffe

Many people live in Africa.
Many animals live in Africa too.
Africa is their home.

stripes

zebra

grass

Zebras are wild.
Zebras have black and white stripes.
These zebras are eating grass.

Lions are wild.
Lions are big cats.
Lions eat zebras and other animals.
This lion is roaring.

Ostriches are wild.
Ostriches are big birds.
An ostrich cannot fly.
This ostrich is running.

Hippos are wild.
Hippos like the water.
The water keeps them cool.
This hippo is swimming.

ear

trunk

Elephants are wild.
Elephants have long trunks and
floppy ears.
This elephant is walking.

Many animals live in Africa.
Africa is their home.
Can you name some of them?